WITH ANGER
by Dr. Lawrence J. Crabb, Jr.

A MINISTRY OF THE NAVIGATORS
P.O. BOX 6000, COLORADO SPRINGS, COLORADO 80934

The Navigators is an international Christian organization. Our mission is to reach, disciple, and equip people to know Christ and to make Him known through successive generations. We envision multitudes of diverse people in the United States and every other nation who have a passionate love for Christ, live a lifestyle of sharing Christ's love, and multiply spiritual laborers among those without Christ.

NavPress is the publishing ministry of The Navigators. NavPress publications help believers learn biblical truth and apply what they learn to their lives and ministries. Our mission is to stimulate spiritual formation among our readers.

The content of this booklet is adapted from *THE MARRIAGE BUILDER* by Lawrence Crabb, Jr., Copyright 1982 by Zondervan Corporation. Used by permission. To fully benefit from the author's message, the reader is encouraged to enjoy a complete reading of *The Marriage Builder*, which is available through Christian bookstores.

All Scripture quotations in this publication are from the *Holy Bible: New International Version* (NIV), Copyright © 1973, 1978, 1984, International Bible Society, used by permission of Zondervan Bible Publishers.

Printed in the United States of America

6 7 8 9 10 11 12 13 14 15 16 17 / 99 98 97

HOW TO DEAL WITH ANGER

Fred arrives home after a tough day at work. Unconsciously, he's hoping for a friendly greeting, a warm hug, and a prepared dinner from his wife, Joan. But as he enters the kitchen, Joan turns and asks, "Why are you so late? You said you'd be home by six and it's nearly seven!" Fred's teeth clench and his eyes blaze as half a dozen possible responses flash through his brain. Fred is angry.

Fred is mad because Joan has blocked his goal—affection. Everything we humans do has a goal. We are not the victims of internal, psychological forces that drive us in unwanted directions. Although it may often *feel* as though we do things we don't want to do, in truth our every action is an attempt to reach a goal that deep down makes good sense to us. When a goal is blocked, it's normal to feel mildly frustrated or furious, depending on how important the goal seems.

As his blood pressure rises, Fred (like most of us) is asking himself, *What should I do?* His options are (1) to express his anger, (2) to defend his late arrival, (3) to ignore Joan's comment and wash up for dinner, or (4) to soothe her with an apology and a warm embrace. However, God is less concerned with Fred's specific *behavior* than with his *motives*. The question Fred needs to ask is not "What should I do?" but *"What should be my goal?"*

Stuffing and Dumping

Two opposing approaches to feelings are vying for dominance in our society. On the one hand, many Christians hold that expressing negative emotions is always sinful. Instructions like "You should never be angry" or "If you can't say something nice, say nothing" bind people into straitjackets of emotional denial. People pretend they feel one way, when they really feel quite different. The masks remain rigidly in place, glued on tightly by the belief that Christian relationships must always consist of accepting smiles and warm expressions of love. In fact, the masks cover a Pandora's box of hurt and anger. The goal of this approach is supposedly to avoid hurting the other person, but it generally conceals deeper goals: to protect oneself from conflict or to appear spiritually mature. These deeper goals end up taking precedence over goals like honesty, intimacy, and openhearted ministry to the other person.

On the other hand, some secularists—blissfully ignoring biblical injunctions to put off malice and be kind to one another—insist that feelings are neither good nor bad, they just *are*. For them, the wisdom of expressing emotions is measured not in moralistic terms, but by pragmatism: "Will I feel better if I express myself?" or "I have a right to tell you how I feel. I will do so if I want to." The goal of this strategy is to make me feel good.

Two alternatives confront us: (1) we can *stuff* our feelings inside, or (2) we can assertively *dump* them on others. The first option will produce at best an anxious spiritual phony, and at worst someone who erupts in fits of temper or a bad case of colitis. The second option will avoid psychosomatic illnesses and unexpected outbursts of anger, but at the cost of humility, love, and respect for the other person. Neither strategy is consistent with what I find in the Bible.

Ezekiel 24 is a clue to how God views emotional expression. God told Ezekiel that He was about to take the life of his dearly beloved wife.

> The word of the LORD came to me: "Son of man, with one blow I am about to take away from you the delight of your eyes. Yet do not lament or weep or shed any tears. Groan quietly; do not mourn for the dead." (Ezekiel 24:15-17)

5

The death of a beloved wife is naturally a time for profound grief. But God told His servant to "groan quietly."

First, *God acknowledged that Ezekiel would feel real emotions*. He did not tell the man to feel anything other than what he did feel. Humans are incapable of changing emotions at will. We have just two sets of choices: (1) we can acknowledge them or pretend they don't exist, and (2) we can express or not express them. God told Ezekiel to groan—to acknowledge how he felt, to experience inwardly the weight of a painful response to a pain-producing event.

Ezekiel's grief was not sinful; it was fully consistent with love for God and compassion for others. Some emotions (e.g., jealousy, greed, lust) are sinful in that they block compassion. But both kinds of emotions need to be fully acknowledged before the Lord in different ways. When I experience a nonsinful but painful emotion, I am to come to the Lord fully expressing my feelings in humble dependence on His comfort and sufficiency. When I experience sinful emotions, however, I must approach Him with contrition and repentance, trusting in His forgiveness and His promise to complete the work begun in me. I should openly experience my feelings in humble confession. This does not consist of superficial prayers like "Oh, Lord, please forgive me for being angry." Rather, I will cry, "God I am furious! I am livid with rage! And I know I am wrong! I want to go Your way and be filled with compassion, but right now I am bitter. Please forgive me! I commit myself to Your purposes." This prayer neither denies nor even minimizes the emotion, so it prevents both the phoniness and the ulcers caused by suppressing feelings.

Second, *God instructed Ezekiel to deny himself any public expression of his private grief.* Ezekiel was to acknowledge inwardly how he felt ("groan"), but not express this outwardly ("quietly"). Remember our two sets of choices? Ezekiel was to acknowledge, but not express.

God had a reason for this instruction: the absence of mourning customs would shout to an apostate nation that an impending judgment would be so severe that by comparison a wife's death justified no tears at all.

Thus, God's command to "groan quietly" yields two abiding principles. When an emotion arises within us, we are to:

> • Acknowledge to ourselves and to God how we feel, letting ourselves experience inwardly the full weight of our emotions;
> • Subordinate the public expression of our feelings to the goal of letting God use us for His purposes.

This is the biblical strategy between dumping feelings (which disregards God's purposes) and suppressing feelings (which denies that

God is gracious enough to accept us as we are). The goal of both honesty and selective expression is honoring God.

Goals and Desires

Once we've decided to first acknowledge, then selectively express emotions, our task is to figure out *when* expressing emotions serves God's purpose. Before we can do this, we have to understand the difference between goals and desires.

Every human being longs for security and significance.

The security of relationship
We long for an awareness of being unconditionally and totally loved without needing to change in order to win love—loved by a love that cannot be earned and so cannot be lost.

The significance of purpose
Each person longs for a certainty that he is engaged in a responsibility that is truly important, that its results will not evaporate with time but will last through eternity, that has an important impact on another person, and for which he is fully adequate.

Most of us try either to suppress our longings or to satisfy them through achievement or other people. We try to use earning power, social skills, or ministry talents to win people's approval or make ourselves feel we have an impact on the world. We get angry when people don't respond to our cues to say, "Great job! I appreciate you. I accept you just the way you are. I'm glad you're here." We get mad when people treat us as insignificant or fail to show the love we think they ought to show us.

But we are designed so that only God can meet these needs. The Cross is God's guarantee that He loves us securely and unconditionally. God loves us with a love we never deserved, a love that sees everything ugly within us yet accepts us, a love we can do nothing to increase or decrease.

> You see, at just the right time, when we were still powerless, Christ died for the ungodly. Very rarely will anyone die for a righteous man, though for a good man someone might possibly dare to die. But God demonstrates his own love for us in this: While we were still sinners, Christ died for us. (Romans 5:6-8)

> "Never will I leave you; never will I forsake you." (Hebrews 13:5)

> How great is the love the Father has lavished on us, that we should be called children of God! (1 John 3:1)

Likewise, the Holy Spirit is God's equipment to fulfill tasks in life that contribute to His eternal Kingdom. Every believer is uniquely gifted to build up the Body of Christ in some special, crucial way.

> Now to each one the manifestation of the Spirit is given for the common good. . . . Now the body is not made up of one part but of many.
> If the foot should say, "Because I am not a hand, I do not belong to the body," it would not for that reason cease to be part of the body. . . . If one part suffers, every part suffers with it; if one part is honored, every part rejoices with it. Now you are the body of Christ, and each one of you is a part of it. (1 Corinthians 12:7,14-15,26-27)

> For we are God's workmanship, created in Christ Jesus to do good works, which God prepared in advance for us to do. (Ephesians 2:10)

So, if we have accepted Christ's death for our sins and have received His Spirit into our lives to rule us, then our real needs are fully met.

With our real needs met, God has given us a task that should be the goal of our lives: *to be His chosen instruments by which He touches other's needs*. I call this the goal of ministry. Jesus called it the second greatest commandment: "Love your neighbor as yourself" (Matthew 19:19).

The more time we spend openly communicating with God in prayer and hungrily absorbing what He says in His Word, the more we will be able to believe that He has met our needs. These pursuits are essential. But no matter how much time we spend at them, we will still feel an unquenchable *desire* for people to make us feel loved and significant.

God intends for Fred to feel keenly the effects of the way Joan treats him. God made humans in His image—personal beings with the ability to affect each other profoundly. Without the desire for each other's love, we would be incapable of receiving another person's acceptance with real joy. If we wall ourselves off from intimate relationships, because we need nobody but Christ, then we are rejecting a Godmade desire. But this *desire must never become our goal*.

Let a circle represent our need for longings and significance. Let an outer circle represent our legitimate desire for richly feeling secure and significant in our relationships.

Christ is adequate to meet our needs; He is able to fill the inner circle of the sketch. He has never promised, however, to fill the outer circle of desire. Yet all our longings for warmth, kindness, understanding, respect, and faithfulness from our spouses, parents, children, friends, and coworkers are in that outer circle.

When these desires remain unmet, we feel valid pain. Something good is missing. But because our need to be a worthwhile person is met in Christ whether we feel it or not, we can choose to maintain the goal of ministering to someone who fails to meet our desires.

To define terms: *A goal is an objective that is under my control.* A Christian can make a goal of seeking to minister to others because his needs are met in Christ. (He still needs God's grace to achieve that goal, but it is available to him.) An unbeliever lacks this source of security and significance, as well as this source of empowering grace, so he cannot pursue the goal of ministry in a way that pleases God.

A desire is an objective that I may legitimately and fervently want, but cannot reach through my efforts alone. To fulfill a desire requires another's cooperation.

Fred's feeling of anger is a valuable warning: his goal when he entered his home was manipulative. He was demanding a response from Joan that would meet what he felt to be a need for love. But love from Joan should have been his desire not his goal, because he could not control what Joan did and because his need for love is met in Christ. By acknowledging his feeling, Fred can receive this warning and repent of his wrong goal. Now he can choose a new goal that follows God's purpose: to be God's instrument to express love to Joan.

Perceiving an objective as a goal or as a desire greatly affects what we do with it. My objective may be that it rain this afternoon. If I perceive this as a goal, I will seek some way to make it happen. But since I cannot control whether it rains, I will feel frustration and anger. However, if I perceive it as a desire, I will simply pray that the One who is in control will provide rain. I will also ask myself if I have any real goal that I can do something about. My lawn may be parched. I *desire* that it rain, but my *goal* is that my lawn receive water. I can choose to buy a sprinkler to water the lawn. I may not want to drive to the store and spend the money, but assuming I have the time and the cash, I can choose to do so.

The proper response to a desire, then, is *prayer*. To a goal, the proper response is a set of *responsible actions*. If we confuse goals and desires, our responses will be wrong. Too many people pray about their goals ("Lord, make me treat my wife more kindly") and assume responsibility for their desires ("Honey, will you get off my back?").

Express or Not Express?

But the question remains: Should Fred tell Joan how he feels?

If Fred responds to Joan's accusing question with an expression of irritation ("Hey,

13

after a tough day, I wouldn't mind a smile"),
his goal is to hurt her or to stop her from
complaining or to generate enough guilt to
make her change. None of these motives is
consistent with the goal of ministry. They are
manipulative and therefore sinful. Instead, he
can do the following.

Be slow to anger.
The Scriptures repeatedly exhort us to be care-
ful when we feel angry. It is easy to express our
irritation quickly for the wrong purpose and
thereby sin.

Acknowledge anger.
Fred doesn't need to pretend his emotion isn't
there in order to avoid expressing it in an
uncontrolled and hurtful way. In fact, acknowledging it frankly to God can help him control
his response to Joan.

Think through goals.
Anger generally results when a goal is blocked.
Fred should ask himself what objective he is
seeking. If Joan can block it, then it should
never have been a goal. He needs to relabel it
as a desire ("I hope Joan greets me warmly")
and to reaffirm his commitment to the goal of
ministry.

Deal with desires.
Fred must embrace, not refuse, the pain he
feels because Joan treated him unlovingly. He

can ask God to enable Joan to understand his feelings and treat him better. He can pray for help not to let his hurt color his response to Joan. He can thank God for fully meeting his need for love. If Joan repeatedly hurts him, Fred may have to spend a lot of time pouring out his pain to God and crying out for grace.

Assume responsibility for the proper goal.
Fred must now decide what action he can take to minister to his wife. The goal of ministry always takes precedence over sharing the hurt from thwarted desires. Fred could express understanding of her irritation ("Honey, I can understand that you're angry because I messed up your dinner plans") and show appreciation for her hard work ("I really appreciate the work you put into meals and everything else").

Express negative feelings if doing so serves a good purpose.
At this point (whether two minutes or two hours later), Fred may tell Joan how annoyed he was with the way she greeted him. He should confess his bitter spirit in order to remove any wall of retreat caused by his anger. He may also express his anger, if he judges that doing so will help her better understand how her behavior affects him. If she wants to minister to him (as he desires), then his sharing how he feels when she behaves in a certain way will help her better reach her goal of ministry.

If Fred expresses his negative feelings, after carrying out the other steps, with the purpose of keeping bitterness from taking root or of making himself more understandable and vulnerable to his wife, then the expression of emotion is ministry. Joan may stay angry with him; she may consign him to an evening of hostile neglect or incessant complaint. Fred cannot control what she does. If she responds in continued anger, she is sinfully wrong and he will feel hurt and angry. But he is responsible to sustain his commitment to minister to her. His goal in sharing how he feels must never be to exact revenge or to change Joan.

Content in Christ

There is nothing wrong with diligently working on our goals in the hope that our desires will come true. A woman who makes it her goal to treat her husband with respect may well find her desire for openness from him met. But our hearts must never be set on reaching desires. The Bible says to seek first God's Kingdom, to lay up treasures in Heaven—in other words, to set our hearts on the goal of worshiping God, serving Him, and becoming more like Christ. By God's enabling grace, this goal is reachable no matter what our circumstances are.

Paul wrote that he had learned the secret of contentment whether his circumstances were pleasant or painful (Philippians 4:10-13). The secret is, "I can do everything through

16

him who gives me strength" (verse 13). Paul's *goal* was to please the Lord, to become increasingly like his Master. No doubt his *desires* included the freedom to preach in the churches he loved, to fellowship with his brothers and sisters, and to enjoy certain physical comforts. But whether or not his desires were met, he could always accomplish what he had his heart set on—the goal of living for God—and therefore he was content.

Summary

Christ is fully adequate to respond to our longings for security and significance.

Feeling secure and significant because of what other people do is not under our control, and Christ hasn't promised that we will feel these things.

Therefore, our goal in relationships should not be to feel that our needs are met, but to be God's instrument in touching other's needs.

Anger arises when a goal is blocked.

When hurt or anger arises within us, we are to:

- fully acknowledge to ourselves and to God how we feel;
- ask, "What is my goal?"
- deal with desires in prayer;
- assume responsibility for the proper goal;
- express our feelings if doing so serves the goal of ministry.

For Reflection and Action

1. a. What does Luke 15:11-32 suggest about God's love for you?

18

b. Do you have trouble believing this? If so, why?

2. What does God say in these passages about your unique importance in the world?

   Matthew 28:18-20

   John 13:34-35

   Corinthians 12:12-27

3. If Christ meets your needs fully, why should you bother to have intimate relationships in which you are bound to get hurt?

4. How does David express his feelings about other people to God in Psalms 58, 59, and 69?

5. Are you generally more tempted to suppress anger or to dump it all over the other person? Why do you think this is so?

6. Recall a recent time when you were angry with someone.

   a. Tell God exactly how you felt. (It might help to speak aloud or write.)

   b. What goal of yours did the other person block?

   c. Should that have been your goal? (Did it contribute to loving God or others? Was it under your control?)

   d. If you think your goal or the way you treated the other person was wrong, confess your sin to God. Ask His forgiveness.
      Tell God the goal you would like to have in dealing with this person.
      Tell God your desires regarding this person. Ask Him to fulfill those desires and to give you the grace to focus on your true goals.

e. How can you go about meeting your true goal—God's purpose—regarding this person? Prayerfully make some specific plans.

For Meditation

Meditating on Scripture is enormously helpful in changing your goals. Consider reading one of the following passages several times a day until you have memorized it. Post it where you will see it often. What does it say about your needs for love and significance?

"But seek his kingdom, and these things will be given to you as well. Do not be afraid, little flock, for your Father has been pleased to give you the kingdom."
(Luke 12:31-32)

"'My son,' the father said, 'you are always with me, and everything I have is yours.'"
(Luke 15:31)

"Love each other as I have loved you. Greater love has no one than this, that he lay down his life for his friends."
(John 15:12-13)

*I can do everything through him who
gives me strength.   (Philippians 4:13)*

*"Never will I leave you; never will I for-
sake you."   (Hebrews 13:5)*

The NavPress Booklet Series includes:

A Woman of Excellence
by Cynthia Heald

Avoiding Common Financial Mistakes
by Ron Blue

Building Your Child's Self-Esteem
by Gary Smalley & John Trent

Claiming the Promise
by Doug Sparks

Dealing with Desires You Can't Control
by Mark R. McMinn

God Cares About Your Work
by Doug Sherman & William Hendricks

How to Deal with Anger
by Larry Crabb

How to Handle Stress
by Don Warrick

How to Have a Quiet Time
by Warren & Ruth Myers

**How to Keep Your Head Up
When Your Job's Got You Down**
by Doug Sherman

How to Know God's Will
by Charles Stanley

How to Overcome Loneliness
by Elisabeth Elliot

Prayer: Beholding God's Glory

When You Disagree: Resolving Marital Conflicts
by Jack & Carole Mayhall

You Can Trust God
by Jerry Bridges